The Last Meet

Team-mates

Library of Congress Cataloging in Publication Data
Sheffer, H. R.
  The last meet.
  (Teammates)
  SUMMARY: Kurt competes against his best friend for standing in the
pre-Olympic gymnastic trials and also for his girl.
  (1. Gymnastics--Fiction) I. Schroeder, Howard. II. Vista III Design. III.
Title. IV. Series.
PZ7.A1595Las   (Fic)   80-28766
ISBN 0-89686-103-1 (lib. bdg.)
ISBN 0-89686-113-9 (pbk.)

International Standard Book Numbers:
    0-89686-103-1 Library Bound
    0-89686-113-9 Paperback
Library of Congress
Catalog Card Number:
    80-28766

Box 3427
Hwy. 66 South
Mankato, MN 56001

The Last Meet

BY H.R. SHEFFER

ILLUSTRATED BY VISTA III DESIGN

EDITED BY DR. HOWARD SCHROEDER
Professor in Reading and Language Arts
Dept. of Elementary Education
Mankato State University

CRESTWOOD HOUSE

Mankato, Minnesota

The Last Meet

The Madison High gymnasium was set up for the gymnastics team. Horse and parallel bars stood empty and waiting. The steel rings hung from the ceiling, and thick crash pads lay around on the floor.

Kurt Mellon sat cross-legged on one of the mats, idly drumming his fingers on the wooden floor. He was the first team member to arrive for Saturday morning practice.

The door to the gym swung open and Larry Escott burst into the room.

"Hi," he called. "Where is everybody?"

Kurt shrugged. "Beats me. Even the coach hasn't shown up yet."

"Did you take out the chalk and the rosin?" Larry asked.

Kurt reached around behind him on the mat and held up the two containers.

"Okay. Then let's get started."

Larry bent down beside him and rubbed the rosin on the soles of his gymnastic slippers. He rubbed some of the chalk on his hands and went over to the parallel bars. He used a running spring mount, went through a straddle routine, and dismounted with a front somersault. The whole thing was done smoothly and easily.

4

Kurt had watched him without comment. He and Larry were good friends. They had been good friends since the fourth grade. But lately Kurt had noticed something strange; Larry always seemed to be trying to outdo him.

Take this morning, for instance. No gymnast would swing into a move like that without warming up first. But Larry had walked in, said hello, and gone right into a perfect mount, routine, and dismount. That meant he had warmed up someplace. Had he been here earlier and not let on to Kurt that he was in the building?

Kurt shook his head. He didn't understand what was going on between them. He'd been thinking about it a lot lately.

It seemed to him it had all started back when the coach put them on Madison High's gymnastic team. They were both good, almost equally so. Larry had a slight edge in the bar workouts. He was taller than Kurt, and thinner. But Kurt had more strength in his chest and arm muscles. He shone on the steel rings and in the vaulting.

Kurt stood up and went to the exercise mat. He did his warming up with a tumbling routine, something all gymnasts do well. After some beginning stretches he rolled into a series of somersaults, then tried a few cartwheels and handstands.

After the last cartwheel he rested for a moment on the edge of the mat, once again, his brain busy thinking. Could Jody have anything to do with this?

For a moment, a picture of Jody flashed before his eyes, and he smiled to himself. Jody Gray. Five foot nothing, and the cutest girl he'd ever known. She, too, was a gymnast. In fact, she had gone into it because of Kurt's interest in it. And she was good. Her small, agile body looked beautiful swinging on the uneven parallels, sailing over the side horse, and especially arching and twisting through the moves of the floor exercise. Jody was already receiving high marks in team competitions.

Several other team members had come into the gym by now, and in a few minutes Coach Mulligan arrived.

"Sorry I'm late, guys," he said. He clapped his hands together. "Let's get moving."

They started with team drills. First on the side horse, then moving to the parallel bars, the horizontal, and the rings.

Kurt knew that Jody was over in the girls' gym, going through the same routines. The gym team always used the school on Saturdays. It was the one day of the week when the other athletes weren't interested in it. By tonight, the gymnastic equipment would be stored away, the basketball hoop would be lowered again from the ceiling, and the school basketball team would play one of their season games.

When the workout was finished and they had showered and changed, Kurt and Larry left the gym together. Jody was standing in the hall, waiting for them.

"Hi." She smiled, sharing the smile between the two of them. "Ready to leave? Come on over to my house and I'll fix a sandwich."

Kurt wasn't sure if she was talking to both of them or not. But Larry grinned and slipped his arm around Jody's shoulders.

"That sounds great. Let's get going."

Kurt walked along behind, trying to beat down

the feeling that he was getting shoved aside. He had a date with Jody that night. They were supposed to go to the movies. He wondered if she was going to invite Larry along on that, too.

When they got to the Grays' house, Jody's mother invited them to sit down at the kitchen table. She and Jody quickly put together sandwiches and a pitcher of lemonade, then sat down to join the boys.

"How's the gym coming?" Larry asked. "Any new equipment, Jody?"

Jody's father, proud of his daughter's gymnastic ability, had fixed up a gym for her in the basement of the house.

Jody nodded. "We've done a little more on it.

I'll show you after we're through eating."

She helped her mother clear the table, then took them down the basement stairs.

Her mini gym was equipped with regulation crash pads, a horse, and a padded balance beam. There was also a stretch of mat for her to practice her floor exercises, although it was not regulation size.

The balance beam was new. Kurt walked over to it to see how it was padded. It seemed to be a vinyl covering of some kind. He was curious about it. Men gymnasts don't work on a balance beam, but women gymnasts do some of their most difficult work on it.

"It looks great," Larry said. "It should be a big help to you, being able to practice down here, I mean."

"Yes." Jody laughed. "I think my father thinks I'll be walking off with the gold medal in the Olympics."

"Well, why not?" Larry asked. "Somebody has to do it."

"Ha!" Jody laughed. "In the first place, I'm already too old. And besides, I'm happy to just compete with the team. I don't want to be a professional athlete."

Larry raised an eyebrow. "How about you, Kurt?"

Kurt turned around and looked at him. "No,"

he said. "I've never really thought about going that far."

"Well, I have." Larry folded his arms and looked defiant. "I'm getting better every day. The coach says so. I'll probably never make it to Olympic status, but I'm sure going to go as far as I can."

"You mean you're going into the big competitions?" Jody asked.

"That's right," Larry said. "I'm going up to Allentown next month. Aren't you?"

Usually they all competed on the Madison High team. But the following month there was a pre-Olympic competition where they could enroll as individuals and compete against other single gymnasts from their district.

Kurt had had no idea that Larry intended entering on his own. A fee was required for each event in which a gymnast wanted to compete for individual honors.

"What are you going to try for?" Kurt asked.

"Horizontal and parallel," Larry said. "And, of course, floor exercise."

Kurt nodded. Larry was tops on their team in the floor exercise. His long, lean body lent itself well to the movements on the ground. It required a lot of physical strength and a great deal of flexibility and rhythm.

"How about you, Kurt? Why don't you try it with me?"

"Nah, I'm not interested," Kurt said.

"Oh, yes!" Jody clapped her hands. "Why don't you? I think it would be great. The fee isn't that high, and you're so good on the rings. Why don't you try just this once?"

Kurt stopped for a moment. He'd never even thought about going in for individual competition. But if Jody wanted him to —

"Are you going to compete?" he asked her.

"Me?" Her eyebrows shot into the air. "No

way! You couldn't pay me to do it. I don't mind working with the team, but that's it. But you — " She touched Kurt's arm. " — You're great. And as long as Larry's going to do it, I think you should, too."

He shrugged her off. "What's Larry got to do with me?" he asked.

Jody moved back a step and he saw a look of surprise flash across her face.

"Why, nothing, of course," she said. "I just thought, well, if you wanted to do it — " Her voice trailed away.

Kurt gritted his teeth. What was the matter with him? He was reading all kinds of things into something that probably didn't mean anything.

"I'll think about it," he replied. "Listen, I have to go. I've got things to do this afternoon. Uh, we still have a date tonight, don't we?"

"Of course we have a date," Jody said. "You asked me, didn't you?"

"Okay. I'll be here at eight. You coming, Larry?"

"Yeah. I'll be right with you."

Kurt ran up the cellar stairs. He could hear Larry saying something to Jody down below, but he couldn't catch what they were saying. Then he heard Larry's footsteps coming up behind him and he yanked open the kitchen door, walking out into the cold February afternoon air.

All that evening Kurt kept waiting for Jody to mention Larry's name. But she didn't. Finally, after the movie and a hamburger at the local burger joint, Kurt drove her home, parking in front of her house. The porch light was on but inside it was dark.

"Do you want to come in?" she asked.

"If it's okay with your folks," he said.

"Sure. They don't mind."

She used her key to open the front door and led him into the kitchen.

"Do you want a glass of milk, or something?" she asked.

"No, thanks. I've had enough," Kurt said. "Can we sit down someplace?"

"Sure."

He followed her into the den. She turned on a lamp in the far corner, leaving the rest of the room in semi-darkness.

Kurt sat down next to her on the sofa, slipping his arm around her waist. He leaned over and kissed her.

Jody pulled back, gasping a little, laughing. He grinned back at her. Everything seemed a lot better now.

But it didn't last long.

"What do you think of Larry signing up for the individuals?" she asked, spoiling his mood completely. "I never dreamed he was thinking of something like that."

Kurt slumped back in the corner of the sofa. "Do you really care whether he enters or not?"

"Of course I do!" she said. "He's good. And so are you. That's why I think you should go into it, too."

"Uhm," he grunted. "I'll think about it." He moved back next to her. "Do we have to talk about this now?"

She smiled and leaned against his shoulder. "Not if you don't want to. But I thought it was great that he'd even think of such a thing."

"Yeah," he said. "Well, he's a terrific guy."

"Yes." She shook her head. "He really is."

Kurt stared down at her for a moment. He hadn't exactly meant it that way.

"You will think about it, Kurt, won't you? About going into the individuals, I mean?"

"Sure." He sighed. "I'll think about it. But I'm not promising anything."

He did think about it all the next day. Finally, he asked his father what he thought.

"It's up to you, Kurt," his father said. "You and the coach. Have you said anything to Coach Mulligan?"

"No. I'd never thought about it myself until yesterday when Larry said he was going to do it."

"Well, it certainly can't hurt," his mother added. "As long as it doesn't mean life or death to you, it might be fun to compete individually once in a while."

"Kurt, you don't have any ideas about some-day being a champion, do you? I mean, in the Olympics or anything like that?" his father asked.

"Why not?" Kurt was suddenly defensive. "That's what Larry's talking about."

"Hey, if you want it," his father said, "that's great. But don't forget, I've known you all your life. You've never had that kind of ambition before."

"Well, maybe I've got it now."

"Maybe you do," His father said. "But if you do, I'm wondering if you have it for the right reasons."

Kurt stared at him for a moment, then turned on his heel. "I'm going up and do homework," he said.

What kind of reasons were the right reasons? If Larry could do it, he could, too; that was reason enough.

During the week there were no gymnastic workouts after school, since the basketball team tied up the gym floor. But there was one period during the school day when they were able to use the gym.

Kurt mentioned the idea of his competing in Allentown to Coach Mulligan. The coach thought it was a good idea. He thought Kurt might have a chance at winning a competition medal.

"How many events are you going to enter?" the coach asked.

"Well, the rings for sure," Kurt said, and the coach nodded.

"Yes, that's your best event. But I think you

should enter another one, too. How about the long horse?"

"Okay."

"And the floor exercises," the coach said.

Kurt frowned. "I'm not that good at it."

"Sure you are," the coach added. "You may not be as flexible as Larry, but there's a lot of strength in your movements. That counts for points, too. Besides, you're not planning on winning all three events, are you?" The coach grinned at him.

"Nah." Kurt smiled back. "I may not win any of them. But, it'll be fun."

He started working on his floor exercise routine that day. Because this was a pre-Olympic meet, there were strict rules to be followed.

During the floor exercise he had to do five easy moves, five medium ones, and one movement of superior difficulty. They were called A for easy ones, B for medium, and C for the hardest.

Kurt decided to use the regular opening — a series of handsprings and roundoffs, ending at the diagonal corner with a high somersault. The high somersault would meet the requirement for a C movement. He would then work his way down one side of the mat to the third corner and move

diagonally across to the fourth corner. The basic requirement in floor exercise was that the gymnast
must use the entire mat during the routine.

Kurt began putting together a routine of single
front somersaults and single back somersaults,
mixed with handsprings and other forms of tumbling.

When school was over that day, he couldn't find Jody anywhere. He was beginning to get excited about the idea of competing as a single, and he decided to go over to her house and see if he could practice down in the basement. He needed to work on his vaulting, especially the handsprings and the handstand cartwheels.

When he got to the Grays' house, Mrs. Gray told him Jody was in the basement.

"Larry Escott is with her," Mrs. Gray said. "I believe they're practicing."

Kurt thanked her and started down the basement stairs. He saw them right away. Larry had his arms around Jody and was kissing her warmly.

Kurt felt anger building inside him. That was his

girl Larry had his hands on. He clattered down the rest of the stairs, making as much noise as he could. The pair below broke apart and Kurt could see that Jody looked angry.

Larry stared at him. "What are you doing here? We didn't expect you."

Kurt lowered his head, looking away. "I came to practice," he muttered.

He threw off his jacket, ripping off his shirt and jeans, revealing his gym shorts underneath. Jody and Larry both had their gymnastic uniforms on.

Kurt swung himself up on the horse and began doing a complicated series of leg scissors.

"Aren't you going to warm-up?" Jody asked. She stood in front of him, hands on hips, looking at him.

"Nope," he said through clenched teeth.

"Did you ever think of asking me if I mind if you use the equipment?" she asked.

He sat down on the horse. "Do you want me to leave?"

Her face reddened. "No. Of course not."

She turned and walked over to the mat and began doing her stretching exercises. Larry joined her.

For a few moments there was silence in the basement except for the grunts as they stretched their muscles and the slapping against the horse as Kurt once more went into his scissor routine.

He could see that Jody and Larry were thinking about themselves and ignoring him. The anger inside him built up more and more. As it grew, his legs moved faster and faster. He could feel the muscles pulling inside his thighs. It really had been stupid not to warm-up first. He was cold, and he knew it.

He saw Jody look at him out of the corner of

her eye and he immediately began doing a long series of double scissors along the horse.

When the pain hit him, it was bad. It felt as if someone had reached in and ripped the tendon right out of his leg. He let out a cry and slid from the pommel down to the mat below. Jody and Larry ran over to see what was wrong. Kurt sat holding his leg.

"Well, that was stupid!" Jody raged. "I told you to warm-up first."

Kurt grabbed the iron leg of the horse and pulled himself up.

"Come on. I'll help you get home," Larry said.

"No, thanks." The pain in his leg was terrible. He could hardly get up the stairs. He didn't know how he'd drive the car, but he wouldn't let Larry help him.

When he finally got home, he limped slowly up the walk to the house. No one was there. He made his way painfully up the stairs to his bedroom, flopping across the bed with relief.

For some reason, the leg seemed to hurt more when he was lying down. He finally eased the pain by putting a pillow under his knee. He was afraid to think of what he might have done. If it was only a pull, he'd be all right in a week or so. But if he had torn the tendon, it would take months to heal. Right now it felt as if he'd yanked his whole leg apart. And the worst part of it was that it needn't have happened at all. It was his own fault, trying to show off in front of Jody, trying to show her he was better than Larry.

By the next afternoon the leg had been x-rayed and Kurt knew the damage was not serious. But it would be at least a week before he could begin to exercise the leg again. There would be very little time for him to practice a decent routine for the Allentown meet. The doctor told him to stay off the leg for a couple of days. Then he could go back to school as long as he didn't do anything to strain the leg.

The following afternoon Jody arrived with his school books and homework assignments. She sat in a chair next to his bed and gave him a funny kind of look.

"What did you think you were doing?" she finally asked.

He shrugged. "Showing off, I guess."

She turned her head to the side. "That isn't like

you. You've been acting pretty strange the last week or so."

"So have you," he said.

She reached across and took his hand. "You saw Larry kissing me, didn't you?"

He sighed and pulled his hand away, swinging his arm over his head, staring up at the ceiling.

"You can kiss anybody you want."

Jody slumped in her chair. "You're being very difficult, Kurt." Her voice was so low he could hardly hear her.

He sat up and propped himself against the back of the bed. "Are you dating him?"

Jody shook her head. "No. And I didn't mean to kiss him, either. It just sort of happened."

Kurt asked, "How does something like that sort of happen?"

Anger blazed in her eyes. "He sort of grabbed me, that's how it happened."

Kurt frowned. "You mean you didn't want him to?"

Jody got up and came over to sit next to him on the bed. "I know Larry is your best friend. But I don't think that matters to him when it comes to girls."

Kurt suddenly felt a million times better. He smiled. "I think you're right."

Jody leaned over and kissed him lightly on the cheek. "Is everything okay now?"

He squeezed her hand. "Sure."

"Okay. I'm going to leave so you can do your homework. As soon as the doctor says it's all right, why don't you come down to the basement and start doing some easy stuff?" Her eyes sparkled and she put her hands on her hips. "And I do mean easy!"

That Saturday Kurt went to watch the gymnastic workout, but didn't take part. It wasn't until the following Wednesday that his leg felt well enough for him to do anything.

After school that day he met Jody and they went back to her house. He started with the easiest of the warming up exercises, doing a slow routine, testing the leg at every move. It seemed to be fine.

By Saturday he was back on the rings.

"Stick to that for today," the coach said. "You need to get your arms in shape and it shouldn't bother the leg at all."

It didn't. He swung through a routine of chinups, bird's nest, back uprises, reverse kicks, and flying wings. Even his iron cross was good, although he could see that the rings were moving slightly.

"Leave the floor exercise for another few days," the coach said. "Give the leg a full chance to heal."

"What about the horse?" Kurt wanted to know.

"Try it," the coach said. "But try it gently. Think more about your form than speed or height."

Kurt did as the coach suggested. It seemed to work fine.

It was only ten days now until the Allentown meet. Kurt had been watching Larry during his workouts. He was great on the horizontal bars. His body seemed to have been built for that kind of ex-

ercise. He showed a long, graceful line in every movement. Kurt knew he would do well in the competition.

Now it became a burning desire with Kurt. He had to score high in at least one of his stunts. The only stunt that he and Larry were both signed up for was the floor exercises. He wanted to do it there.

That week he went to Jody's every day to practice. He did his work on the rings and the horse during the gym period at school. At Jody's he practiced only the floor work. There wasn't enough room to do a full routine, but there was space for the flip flops. He wanted to do something really great — a double full twist or a back with a full twist. He practiced them for a long time.

The last Saturday before the meet he put the whole routine together in the gym in front of the coach. When he was finished, the coach stared at him.

"Don't you think that's a bit too much?" he finally asked. "You've got three C's in there, three of the hardest movements. You only need one."

"I know," Kurt said. "But I want to do it that way."

"Sometimes that doesn't sit too well with the judges," the coach said. "It looks a bit like showing off, if you know what I mean."

Kurt paused. He knew the coach was right. But somehow he had to do something to take the first away from Larry.

He had been watching Larry on the floor. Larry didn't have the power in his arms and back that Kurt had, but he had the grace and movement that stand out in the floor routine.

"I think I'll leave it the way it is unless you tell me not to," Kurt said.

The coach shrugged. "It's your routine. You have to do it your own way." He started to leave. "By the way, it's very good."

He smiled at Kurt and walked away.

By the time they got to Allentown the following week, Kurt had the whole routine down pat.

Larry and Kurt both did well. Larry took a first in the horizontal bars and a third in the parallel. Kurt took two seconds in the rings and the horse. Then it was time for the floor exercise.

Numbers were drawn for order of appearance. Larry was second. Kurt was eighth, almost the last one to perform.

Larry's routine went well. His timing was slightly off, but his form was tops, and the judges gave him good ratings.

When it finally came to Kurt's turn, Larry was still the one to beat. Kurt stood in the corner, ready to begin. The coach stood behind him. Although he could not speak to them while they were doing the routine, he was allowed to stand at the edge of the mat and watch.

Just as the judge gave him the starting signal, Kurt saw Jody sitting on the bench with the rest of the team. She smiled and blew him a kiss. Suddenly it didn't make any difference what Larry had done. It didn't make any difference whether he beat him or not. He was just going to do the best that he could. If he won, fine, and if he didn't, well, what the heck. He had never really wanted to get into this competition in the first place.

The signal came and he went into his beginning routine of handstands and roundoffs. He ended it with the high vault and moved back up the side with a series of flip flops. But instead of the difficult C parts, he quickly did the easier single fronts and single backs. There was no point now in risking another injury. He knew the routine was going well; he could feel it.

When he finished with a beautiful handspring

and split, he knew he had done better than ever before. As he got up and walked off the mat, the coach smiled at him but raised an eyebrow.

"What happened to all the fancy things?" he asked.

Kurt grinned. "I decided I didn't need them."

And he was right. When his score was announced, he had passed Larry. He had won the first.

He sat down next to Jody on the bench.

"It was great," she said. "I've never seen you perform like that."

"I never felt like this before."

He wondered how he could explain to her what had happened.

Larry came up and slapped him on the shoulder. "Not bad," he said. "But I'll get you next time."

"Next time!" Kurt looked up at him. "What are you talking about?"

"There's a meet in April in Bonnersville. I think we should enter."

Kurt shook his head, laughing. "Forget it, Larry. I've had enough competition. I suddenly realized today that I got into this thing for all the wrong reasons. But I tell you what — Jody and I'll come and cheer for you every time you compete."

He stood up and pulled Jody up beside him. Then he put his arm around her shoulder and they walked away.

Teammates is suspense, romance, and sports.

Enjoy the entire series:

Weekend in the Dunes
Street-Hockey Lady
Winner on the Court
Second-String Nobody
Partners on Wheels
Moto-Cross Monkey
Sarah Sells Soccer
Swim for Pride
Two at the Net
The Last Meet